MW01243619

5 Minute Gratitude Journal for Kids!

I Can Do Anything I Put My Mind To!

Copyright © 2021 Four Sisters Publishing, a Keestar Media Company

All rights reserved.
No part of this book may be reproduced in any form or by any electronic or mechanical means, including information storage and retrieval systems, without written permission from the publisher, except for the use of brief quotations in a book review.

If you would like to use material from this book, prior written permission must be obtained by contacting the publisher at: keekstarmedia@gmail.com

First edition: September 2021
ISBN: 978-1-953268-05-1

This Journal Belongs To:

_____

_____

Introduction Page

You can do anything you put your mind to! Our hope is that this 5 minute gratitude journal will serve as a guide to help grow a positive mind set, and act as a fun tool for self exploration. Remembering what we're thankful for has a strong impact on our health and well being!

Four Sisters
Publishing

All About Me!

Draw a picture of yourself!

Name:

I am

years old.

My favorite color is:

My favorite food is:

My favorite place is:

I love my self because:

Bank of

Affirmations

An act of saying or showing that something is true!

I am smart.
I am brave.
I am strong.
I am kind.
I can do hard things.
Learning is my super power.
I am a problem solver.
I get better at things when I practice.
I am loved.
I am helpful.
I am grateful for everything I have and
all that I get to do.
My mistakes help me learn.
I am a good friend.
I can make a difference.
I believe in myself.
I am creative.
I go after my dreams.
I can do anything I put my mind to!

Naming Our Feelings

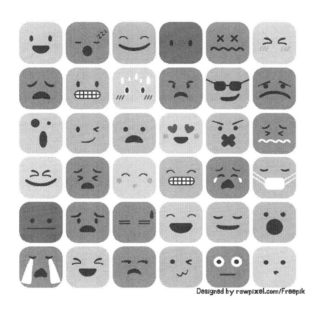

Designed by rawpixel.com/Freepik

Learning to name and become friends with our emotions helps us with our reactions. When we name our feelings it helps us to identify the big emotions we experience. Getting comfortable with our negative feelings can help us too, they can tell us when something isn't right.

Growth Mindset

When You Think This:	Try Thinking This:
I can't do it.	I'm still learning.
I'm not good at this.	How can I get better?
It's good enough.	Did I try my best?
It's too hard.	With practice I will improve.
I'm scared of making a mistake.	My mistakes help me learn.
I'm not as good as them.	What can I learn from them?
I don't know how to do it.	I can learn anything I put my mind to.
I give up.	There are different ways I can try!

Daily Activity

3 things I'm grateful for

Date:

My affirmation today is

Draw how you feel today

Happy

Feeling glad and full of joy!

Daily Activity

2 people I'm grateful for

Date:

Something good that
happened today

Tomorrow I'm looking
forward to

Curious

Excited to investigate. Showing an eagerness to learn.

Daily Activity

3 Things I'm really great at:

Date:

My affirmation today is

Draw how you made someone smile today

Disappointed

Unhappiness from not
getting something
you hoped for.

Daily Activity

The best part of my day was

Date:

My favorite season is

This week will be fun because

Scared

Feeling afraid, fearful, or unsure.

Daily Activity

3 things that make me feel calm

Date:

My affirmation today is

Draw a fun activity you did today

Frustrated

The unhappy
feelings that happen
when you can't do something
you want to do.

Daily Activity

Today I am grateful
for my friend _____ because

Date:

This weekend
will be fun because

I am excited for

Grateful

Focusing on what's good in our lives and being thankful for the things we have.

Daily Activity

3 people I have fun with

Date:

My affirmation today is

Draw a fun moment from today

Overwhelmed

Feeling upset and having
too many thoughts
and feelings.

Daily Activity

A game or sport I enjoy is

Date:

How does it
feel when you don't win?

What does
winning mean to you?

Grumpy

In a bad mood, cranky or grouchy.

Daily Activity

3 things I look forward to this week

Date:

My affirmation today is

What is something you learned today?

Friendly

Welcoming and
pleasant towards others.
Kind and helpful.

Daily Activity

My favorite season is

Date:

Draw your
favorite animal

Something I
enjoy doing outside is

Determined

When you show you've decided to do something and you will not let anything stop you.

Daily Activity

3 things that make me laugh

Date:

My affirmation today is

What is your favorite joke?

Calm

Feeling peaceful,
quiet, and free
of interruptions.

Daily Activity

Sometimes I feel scared when

Date:

Draw the last
time you felt strong

I feel most calm when

Hungry

When you really want
or crave something.

Daily Activity

3 ways I was helpful today

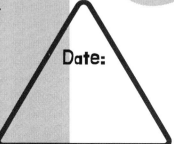

Date:

My affirmation today is

Draw how someone helped you today

Brave

Doing something even
though you're scared.
Showing courage.

Daily Activity

What makes me brave?

Date:

Draw your
favorite superhero

My super power is

AnXiouS

Afraid or nervous
about what may happen.

Daily Activity

3 of my favorite activities are

Date:

My affirmation today is

Draw a memory you are grateful for

Proud

Feeling happy and accomplished for something, someone or your own actions.

Daily Activity

Today I am proud of myself because

Date:

What challenge
did you overcome today?

Tomorrow I'm looking
forward to

Guilty

Feeling responsible for
having done wrong.

Daily Activity

3 people I would like to thank today

Date:

My affirmation today is

In my community I'm thankful for

Energetic

Having big feelings
of energy and action!

Daily Activity

What is your
favorite game to play outside?

Date:

Draw your
favorite season

When I have lots
of energy I like to

Angry

Having a strong feeling of
frustration towards
something or someone.

Daily Activity

3 foods I'm grateful for

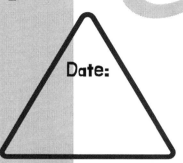

Date:

My affirmation today is

Draw your favorite sweet treat

Loved

To care about or
have warm feelings
towards something
or someone.

Daily Activity

What makes you feel loved?

Date:

Draw someone
who helped you today

How do you show
your family you love them?

Jealous

To want something other people have.

Daily Activity

3 things that make me angry

Date:

My affirmation today is

When I feel upset, how can I calm down?

Embarrassed

Feeling uncomfortable or
confused about your
or someone else's
actions or words.

Happiness Scale

I am a great friend because

Date:

Draw your best friend

I'm grateful
for my friends because

Confident

Trusting yourself, being
sure of your own power!

Daily Activity

3 things that challenge me

Date:

My affirmation today is

Draw how you feel today

Shy

To feel a little scared
when you're around
other people.

Daily Activity

My favorite part about nature is

Date:

Something
I like to do outside

My favorite song

Hopeful

Believing things can be better.

Daily Activity

3 things I'm excited about

Date:

My affirmation today is

A memory that makes me smile

Worried

Feeling a little scared
about something that
may or may not happen.

Daily Activity

The best part about learning is

Date:

My favorite
subject in school

My favorite book

Thoughtful

Showing special care
or thinking carefully
about something or someone.

Daily Activity

3 items I'm grateful for

Date:

My affirmation today is

Draw your favorite toy

Confused

Feeling unsure or not
understanding something
that's happening.

Daily Activity

I felt confused when

Date:

Draw the last
person who helped you

When I learn
from my mistakes I feel

Annoyed

To feel bothered or disturbed.

Daily Activity

3 things that you love about yourself

Date:

My affirmation today is

Draw a picture of you smiling

Silly

To feel playful and
ready to laugh.

Daily Activity

This week I'm thankful for

Date:

Draw a goofy face

What's your favorite joke?

Offended

To feel upset and
angry by something
that was said or done.

Daily Activity

3 friends you like spending time with

Date:

My affirmation today is

What nice things have your friends done for you?

Joy

· Feeling happy
and enjoying yourself!

Daily Activity

What do you think the hardest job in the world is?

Date:

What do you think the best job in the world is?

What do you want to be when you grow up?

Surprised

The feeling you
get when something
unexpected happens.

Daily Activity

3 things you like about school

Date:

My affirmation today is

Draw a picture of your school

Discouraged

When you lose
confidence or excitment.

Daily Activity

My biggest accomplishment last week was

Date:

Draw you silliest face

Who was the
last person to make you laugh?

Content

Wanting no more than
what you have, feeling satisfied.

Daily Activity

3 animals that you love

Date:

My affirmation today is

If you were an animal what animal would you be?

Uncertain

To be unsure of
what is going to happen.

Daily Activity

Happiness Scale

If you could have one superpower what would it be?

Date:

Draw your superpower

Who is your favorite superhero?

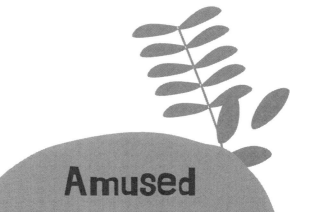

Amused

To feel silly and lighthearted.

Daily Activity

3 things I would like to get better at

Date:

My affirmation today is

Draw the last big project you completed

Sad

To feel unhappy,
upset or dissapointed

Daily Activity

Did anything happen
today that made you upset?

Date:

Draw someone who
always cheers you up

Who do you talk to
when you feel sad?

Tired

Needing rest
and relaxation.

Daily Activity

3 places you would like to visit

Date:

My affirmation today is

Draw a fun memory you have

Excited

Feeling wildly
happy and joyful.

Matching Game

Match the feeling to the definition!

Happy

Curious

Calm

Scared

Confident

Confused

Peaceful, quiet

Unsure,
not understanding

Trusting yourself

Excited,
ready to learn

Glad, full of joy

Afraid or unsure

Matching Game

Match the feeling to the definition!

Embarrassed

Big feelings
and action

Energetic

Uncomfortable
and confused

Thoughtful

To feel bothered

Loved

Too feel playful

Annoyed

Showing
special care

Silly

To care about

Maze

Tick-Tac-Toe

Tick-Tac-Toe

Tick-Tac-Toe

Tick-Tac-Toe

Tick-Tac-Toe

Tick-Tac-Toe

Tick-Tac-Toe

Doodle

Doodle

Doodle

Doodle

Made in the USA
Middletown, DE
01 October 2021

49243790R00057